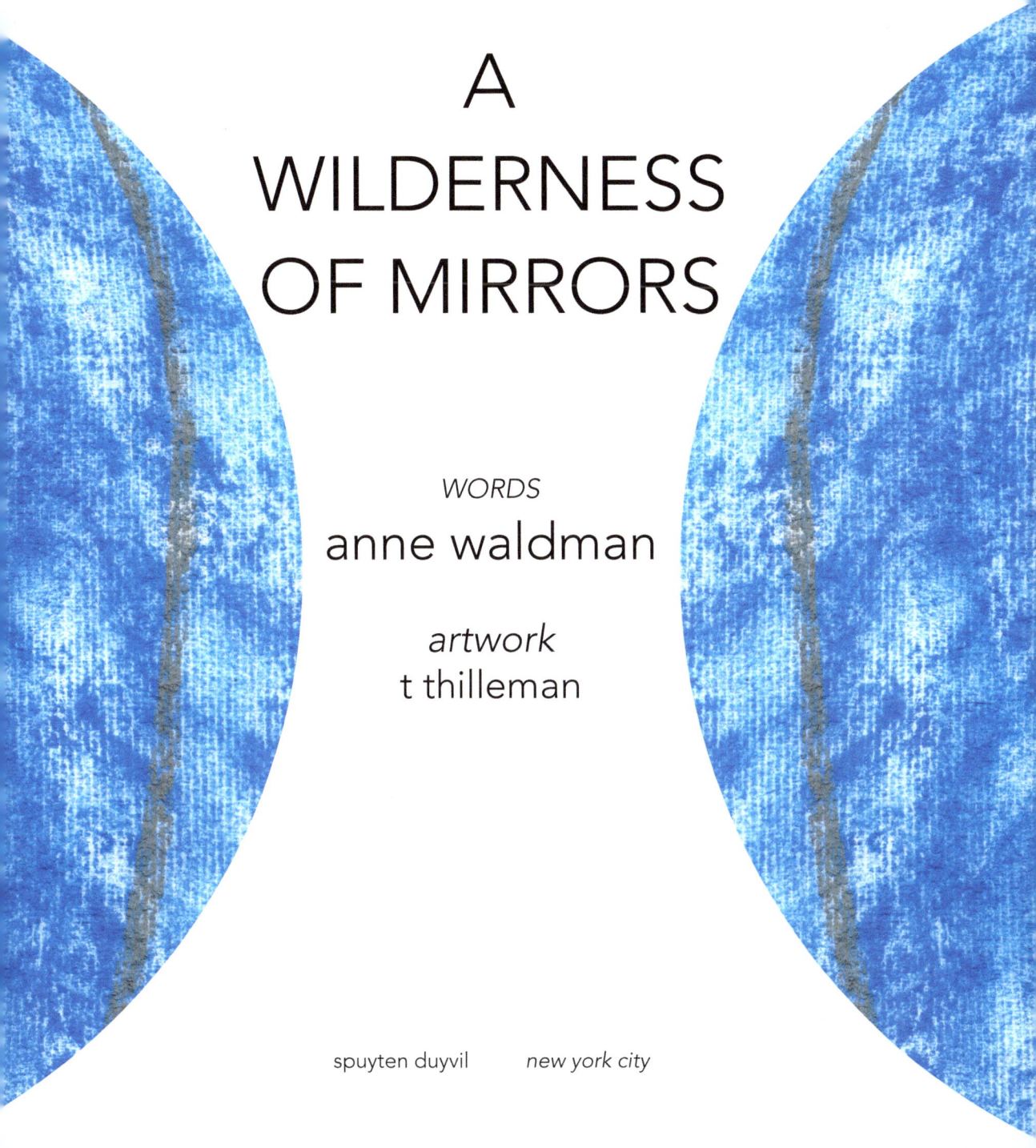

A WILDERNESS OF MIRRORS

WORDS
anne waldman

artwork
t thilleman

spuyten duyvil   *new york city*

goes higher in pitch

advantage of distance,

 and of feminist outrage.

my vocal chords reach high notes.

performatively

 vocal stretch up

 maybe feels like thots

but hotter

they too perform,

   wild movement mind throat

      how are we drawn

into cyclic existence.

            by sound often think

more dynamic   movement

   "perfect hara-chakra-awareness"

outrage

close now,

vertical inanna

happy in her mobile coven.

sitting on a man's head.

"coming after" the multiple guises (!)

that foreground the female, after all
    rather than have her "reified"
as per olson or williams.

she   lost in **their** epics.

but found in her sousveillance.

in   under.

magic all-seeing yab-yum....

                               eyes as doors.

        don't harm language-womb
                         it's fontanelle

how are we zodiac manusya*

=sanskrit : dis interment

discernment

summoned yamantaka

"hummmmm" tibetan for human.

minds   entire   wakened

address the sky jewel adornment as

poets   also   have their labor below the earth

audient

* or manusyagati ="humans" according to the "world of transmigration"
  mahāyāna = behavior of all beings, gods and humans, in death and life alike

the chief demi-gods ketu/rahu*

garland & necklace live at different levels

above the ocean floor.

in hibernation, a praxis of poetry.

variable   williams the baby doctor.

** vedic zodiacal coordinates representative
of head and body, one light the other heavy*

feminist
    or queered consciousness
        in *iovis* wants you to see

where locuter has travelled—

        to the complicated....

cardboard slums or gone lands

....a vow to enter all embrasures which are endless.

keys in hand of mind,

locks slipped…

without notice   you are beckoned   shaky
entering mirage

seduce the weal

you are fearless   you are fearlessly manifested

and dancestomp to atmospheric rattles

the "purposeful overcharges"
of pound williams lawrence as therapeutic.
to attend, to restore?

fever for a day? work the woman's body
as with plough. or as hunter with arrow.

and we would share that "test",

but the feminine principle of makeup

on empty space

seemed absent [in that therapy]

so driven to create a zone,

that allows gestation (gharba)

and generation (bardo)…

what is the arkheion of form

in ephemeros?

what is pulled out of the throat

that you can't see?

what pivots

when you apply the skin, adorned now...

not flayed..

poet becomes: tender

george oppen...

"we must talk now.

i am no longer sure of the words,

the clockwork of the world"

"dark female-enigma"

root of heaven and earth….."

use it: it's **effortless**.
the environment (dharmadhatu)
is always there. holding up

the mirror

in a wilderness of mirrors…

be quivering but very still.

how things appear is my being
how things arise is my reality
there is no phenomenon that is not me
in the whole universe

tt & aw

www.ingramcontent.com/pod-product-compliance
Lightning Source LLC
Chambersburg PA
CBHW041558120626
46551CB00002B/254